QATAR

QATAR

STACEY INTERNATIONAL

The publishers wish to thank the following for their invaluable assistance in the preparation of this book:
H.E. Issa Ghanim al Kuwari, Abdulla M. Sadiq, Nasser al Noaimi, Mustapha al Aydi, Yousuf Mohammad Darwish, Ministry of Information, Doha; Hisham Qaddoumi; Ahmad al Anani; Kamal Rashid; Nasser al Othman; Darwish al Far; Hussein al Fardan; Jassim Zainal; Ali Noaimi; A. Kaye Howard; G. Shaqareq; Jassim al Qattan; Qahtan R. Masri; Leila Fanous; Jumah al Kaabi.

Designed and produced by Stacey International,
128 Kensington Church Street, London W8 4BH
Telex 298768 Stacey G

Editorial
Martin Caiger-Smith

Photography by Robin Clifford,
with the exception of the following:
pp. 4-5, 12 (top), 20-21, 38 (bottom left), 40 (left), 51 (top centre), 54 (left), 55 (bottom right), 59 (right), 64 (top), 66 (bottom right), 67 (bottom), 69 (below left, above and below right), 103, 105 (above and below right), Ministry of Information, Doha; p. 55 (top right), The Studio, Doha; p. 69 (top left), Press Association, London.

Set in Linotronic Plantin by
SX Composing Limited, Essex, England.

Printed and bound by Lund Humphries, London, England.

ISBN 0 905743 43 1

British Library Cataloguing in Publication Data
Qatar.
   1. Qatar – Social conditions
   953'.63053   HN667.A8

STACEY INTERNATIONAL, LONDON

CONTENTS

FOREWORD

THIS BOOK INTRODUCES a country and its people. Such a presentation is appropriate at this time. For Qatar and Qataris have come to stand for a factor for stability, moderation and good sense in a world too often at the mercy of stress and abrupt change.

Qatar may be said to have come to full independence only recently – less than a generation ago. It is relatively small in size and population. And yet its significance is undeniable as a point of stability, of responsibility in this Gulf region, and it sustains a balanced progress.

This would not have been possible but for three fundamental factors – wise and tolerant leadership; racial cohesion; and an abundance of material resources.

The people possess many of the characteristics of a happy family. They have a deep awareness of a common heritage that springs from a sense of belonging to the land, a sincere loyalty to their leadership, and above all a collective commitment to Islam.

His Highness Sheikh Khalifa bin Hamad al Thani,
Emir of the State of Qatar

The Emir of Qatar, His Highness Sheikh Khalifa bin Hamad al Thani, has spoken of Qatar's achievement in terms of a family. "The great efforts of fathers and sons to build a modern nation in which a spirit of brotherhood, justice and equality prevails, constitutes a bright chapter in the history of our people and an illuminating bridge that links the glorious present with the ancient past. This country's renaissance in all fields has been the product of cooperation between the state and the people."

And it is people who are, in His Highness the Emir's words, Qatar's "lasting resource", for oil is recognised as a "depletable asset".

It is the happy collective spirit of its men and women and children that has made today's Qatar an unmistakably contented and harmonious nation, and has accorded its people a thoroughly unified vision of the country they are vigorously building. To Qatar and its people, and those who value man's endeavour for progress, this book is dedicated.

His Highness Sheikh Hamad bin Khalifa al Thani, Heir Apparent, Minister of Defence and Commander in Chief of the Armed Forces

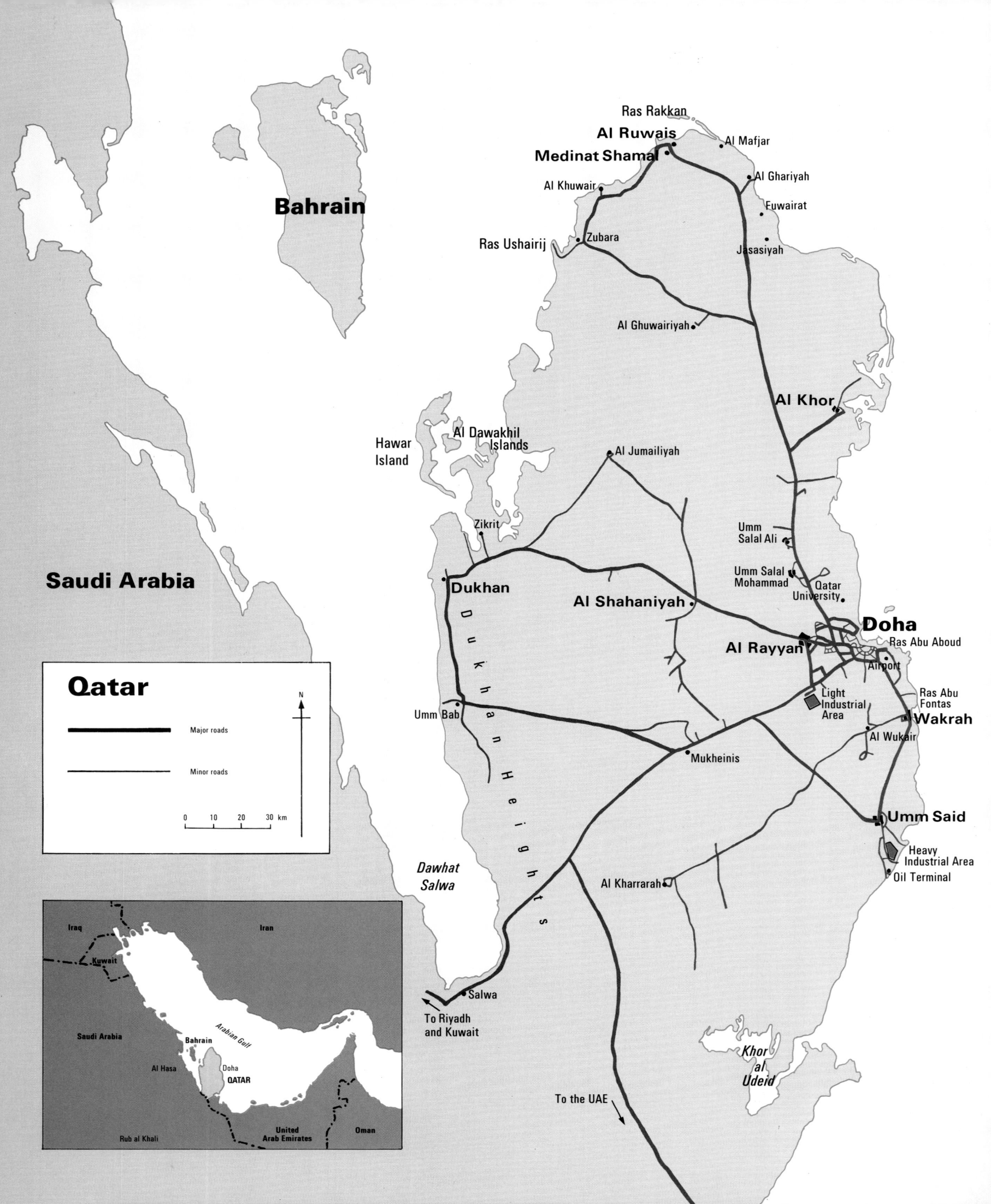

Ras Rakkan

Al Ruwais
Medinat Shamal

Al Mafjar

Al Ghariyah

Al Khuwair

Fuwairat

Ras Ushairij

Zubara

Jasasiyah

Bahrain

Al Ghuwairiyah

Al Khor

Hawar
Island

Al Dawakhil
Islands

Al Jumailiyah

Zikrit

Umm
Salal Ali

Saudi Arabia

Umm Salal
Mohammad

Qatar
University

Dukhan

Al Shahaniyah

Doha

Al Rayyan

Ras Abu Aboud

Airport

Qatar

Ras Abu
Fontas

N

Light
Industrial
Area

Major roads

Wakrah

Al Wukair

Minor roads

Umm Bab

0   10   20   30 km

Mukheinis

Umm Said

Heavy
Industrial
Area

Oil Terminal

*Dawhat
Salwa*

Al Kharrarah

Iraq

Iran

Kuwait

Salwa

*Khor
al
Udeid*

Saudi Arabia

Arabian Gulf

Bahrain

To Riyadh
and Kuwait

Al Hasa

Doha

QATAR

United
Arab Emirates

Oman

To the UAE

Rub al Khali

Dukhan Heights

INTRODUCTION

THOSE RETURNING TO DOHA after a long absence would hardly recognise the city of their memory. Only a few decades ago, the capital, a modest town of low-lying buildings, lay on a half-circle of coastline broken by inlets and dirt roads. Those roads have now been replaced by a wide corniche that follows the line of the bay, flanked with stretches of green, flowers, bushes and palm trees. New buildings tower over it, Ministries, offices and hotels.

During this time, Doha has developed into a modern city, and Qatar has become an independent state, taking its place among the countries of the world. Oil has been a decisive factor in enabling the country to build a stable and prosperous economy, and to achieve one of the highest per capita incomes in the world. The name of Qatar is heard more and more often at world gatherings and conferences, and the young country has its own role to play in regional and international affairs.

Under the Emir Sheikh Khalifa's guiding hand, Qatar's new-found prosperity has brought an astonishing transformation to the country over the last generation, affecting all aspects of Qatari life. Development has been rapid, but always constant, treading that fine line which seeks to absorb the benefits of modern life without sacrificing a distinct national heritage.

The Land

These achievements are all the more striking given the size of the country and its population, terrain and climate. Before the discovery of oil, the land offered its people few natural resources and little material comfort.

The country covers a low-lying limestone peninsula projecting northwards from the western shores of the Arabian Gulf, 11,437 square kilometres in area, 160 kilometres long and 88 kilometres across at its widest. The coastline, which bounds the country to the west, north and east, is 550 kilometres long.

Most is desert terrain. In the north and centre a gravel plain with sparse growth rises towards the west coast, and the ridge known as the Dukhan Heights. To the south, sand dunes encircle the inland gulf of Khor al Udeid. The dunes run on into the *Rub al Khali* ('Empty Quarter'), the vast sand desert which covers much of the Arabian peninsula.

The coastal waters are shallow, and the sandy beaches stretch long at low tide. The coastline is indented with swamps and salt dunes.

Qatar's islands include Halul, eighty kilometres to the east and a centre for oil storage and loading, Hawar, Al Ashat, Janan, Rakan, Mitras and Al Bashiriya.

Summers in Qatar are long, hot and humid, the only relief provided by the prevailing northwesterly winds. Temperatures range from seven degrees centigrade in January to forty-six degrees at the height of summer. Rainfall is slight, averaging some seventy millimetres a year, and is confined to the winter months.

Main towns and villages

Doha, the capital of Qatar, lies halfway along the east coast of the peninsula. Most of the country's population of 270,000 live here, and the city is expanding fast; modern buildings have grown up around the older, traditional ones, and the many mosques boast fine domes and minarets. On the outskirts of the city are the suburbs of Rayyan and Madinat Khalifa, and New Doha, built on land reclaimed from the sea, with sectors for diplomatic missions and modern housing. Doha International Airport lies just outside the city.

Umm Said, where the country's heavy industry is situated, lies forty-five kilometres south of Doha. Its port is the country's main oil export terminal. Industries based south of here include an iron and steel complex, a chemical fertiliser plant, a gas liquefaction plant, an oil refinery and flour mills.

The second largest town in Qatar, **Al Khor**, lies on the coast north of Doha. A narrow bay also known as Khor cuts three kilometres into the coast; the old port serves small vessels and fishing boats.

The old village of **Ruwais** on the northern tip of the peninsula is one of Qatar's most important fishing centres.

Dukhan, the most important oil production centre in Qatar, lies midway down the west coast and was built after the discovery of oil nearby.

South of the Dukhan oilfield, at **Umm Bab**, an oil pipeline complex transfers oil from Dukhan to Umm Said and to the cement plant based there.

Wakrah, between Doha and Umm Said, is famous for its traditional architecture. A small port serves fishing vessels and motorboats.

HISTORY

Excavations in Qatar have provided evidence that the country was inhabited as early as the fourth millenium BC. From the third millenium BC, with the rise of the Mesopotamian civilisation and the founding of the trading centres of Dilmun and Gherra on its western shores, the Gulf became a thriving area of trade and commerce.

Arab historians described the inhabitants of Qatar and surrounding areas as skilled sailors. The Greek historian Herodotus, writing in the fifth century BC, referred to inhabitants of the area as Canaanite tribes. In the 2nd century AD, the geographer Ptolemy recorded a city called Catara on his map of Arabia.

Qatar is famed in Islamic history for the 7th century Arab warrior-poet Qatari Bin Al-Fuja'a. Born in Qatar, he became an outstanding leader, dying far from the land of his birth on one of the Kharijite raids in Persia.

In the eighth century AD, at the time of the Abbasid Empire, the region rose to new heights of prosperity, supplying the wealthy caliphate in Baghdad. An Abbasid settlement has been discovered in Qatar at Murwab on the west coast.

The Portuguese conquered Qatar in 1517, but were driven out by the Ottomans twenty-one years later. The Ottoman Empire incorporated large parts of the Arab world, but its sovereignty over Qatar was seldom much more than nominal.

In the sixteenth and seventeenth centuries, the Gulf region witnessed maritime rivalry between the Portuguese, Dutch, French and British, competing for control of the trade route to India and the Far East.

It was the sea, rather than the land itself, which drew settlers to Qatar. As they grew in number, they established small villages along the eastern and northern shores. Their livelihood came from fishing and pearl-diving, as pearls were found in abundance in the shallow waters of the Gulf. They established trade relations with their neighbours along the Gulf coasts. The first inhabitants paid little heed to the barren interior, which became the domain of bedouin tribes which migrated there in search of water and grazing.

Up until the eighteenth century, there were only five coastal settlements in Qatar: Al Bida (the site of present-day Doha), Wakrah in the south-east, and Huwailah, Fuwairat and Zubara in the north. The eighteenth and early nineteenth centuries saw violent conflicts and bitter struggles to dominate Qatar, during which the coastal villages were threatened and attacked. Finally, Britain imposed the General Treaty of Peace in 1820. However, Qatar remained a non-signatory and its people did not observe the treaty's terms until the bombardment of Doha by the British in 1841.

In 1868, the British Political Resident in the Gulf, Colonel Lewis Pelly, recognised Sheikh Mohammad bin Thani (the great-great-grandfather of the present Emir) as the most influential man in the whole peninsula. Pelly signed a peace treaty with Sheikh Mohammad, as the representative of the people of Qatar. Under the treaty's terms, Sheikh Mohammad was responsible for maritime security. This arrangement only lasted for two years, however, as Qatar came within the sphere of Turkish administration in 1871 following Midhat Pasha's attack on Al Hasa, and the siting of a Turkish garrison in Qatar.

Sheikh Qassim, who succeeded his father Sheikh Mohammad, clashed with the Ottomans over their failure to assist him in settling internal disputes. Open conflict broke out after negotiations between the two sides failed. Sheikh Qassim led the Qataris in an attack on the larger and better armed Ottoman force, winning a victory which is hailed as a landmark in the history of modern Qatar. Sheikh Qassim's authority did much to hasten Qatar's progress towards national unity.

Before the First World War, relations with the British improved. Ottoman influence ended with the conclusion of the Anglo-Turkish Convention of 1913, and Sheikh Abdullah, the son of Sheikh Qassim, supported Britain in the war. Qatar signed an agreement with Britain in 1916 similar to those signed by the other Gulf Emirates, which guaranteed Qatar's security against foreign invasion.

After the First World War, Qatar remained relatively isolated, with a population of 27,000. Most of the inhabitants were poor, especially when their main source of livelihood, pearling, was affected by the drop in world demand and competition from the newly developed Japanese cultured pearl industry.

Spiral rock inscription found at al Kharrara, central Qatar; the only example of its kind found in the lower Gulf. The language is Safaitic Arabic, and the text an invocation to the Nabataean High God MN'T.

Discovery of Oil

In 1923, Sheikh Abdullah received the first request for an exploratory oil concession in the country. World attention was focusing on the likely existence of massive oil reserves in the Gulf area.

Discovery and exploitation of Qatar's reserves was neither rapid nor straightforward. Though the first option was secured in 1926 by the Anglo-Persian Oil Company, it finally expired in 1934 with no concessions yet agreed. Protracted negotiations ensued over the financial and political terms of any such agreement, before the concession was finally signed, in May and June of 1935. The concession was immediately transferred from APOC to Petroleum Development (Qatar) Ltd. Four more years passed before oil was discovered – and though tests carried out at the company's first well in Dukhan in 1940 were successful, the Second World War halted production until 1949.

A new stage had begun in Qatar's life. Production in the Dukhan oilfields increased steadily. A concession to search for offshore oil was awarded in 1952 to the Shell Company; oil was struck and offshore production began there in 1964. After 1974 both offshore and onshore operations came under full state control, and were placed under the supervision of the national authority, the Qatar General Petroleum Corporation (QGPC).

Qatar's oil production revived the country's economy, and Sheikh Abdullah's authority was reinforced and accepted by all. But the enormous task remained of equipping the country to deal with this new industry, and of providing it with an administrative structure and the amenities of the twentieth century.

Qatar, in 1949, lacked all but the most basic elements necessary to constitute a modern state. The country had faced a wave of emigration during the Second World War; its population numbered little more than 25,000, of whom half lived in the small town of Doha. Beyond, villages were small and facilities basic. The vast majority maintained their traditional livelihood, based on fishing, pearling and trading.

The terms set by the oil companies in the concessions were hardly charitable, and revenue, at first, came slowly. Nevertheless, the country began the arduous task of development which has effected so complete a change in Qatar in such a short time. The most urgent priorities were dealt with: provision of fresh water, electricity, and a road network, and first steps towards a complete educational and health system.

Momentum increased in the 1960s as control of administrative affairs fell largely to the Heir Apparent, Sheikh Khalifa bin Hamad al Thani, the present Emir. Under Sheikh Khalifa, a more fundamental plan of development was initiated. Qatar sought to strengthen its links abroad, and a firm basis was laid down for the administrative structure of the new country. As demand increased for labour to participate in this wide-scale development, the population grew as fast as oil production. Social affairs, health and education programmes became a pressing need.

With this rapid progress in the 1960s, Qatar was preparing herself to achieve independent statehood when circumstances were right. Even so, the abruptness of the British decision, in 1968, to withdraw all defence commitments east of Suez by 1971, came as a surprise to Qatar and the other emirates in the lower Gulf. Together, the nine small states sought to safeguard their position by unified action. Qatar itself proposed the creation of a Federation of Arab Emirates at a summit meeting of State Rulers in 1968 but, following lengthy discussions, it became clear that the time was not right for such an idea. After four meetings of the temporary Federal Council in 1968-9, different viewpoints remained. First Bahrain, and then Qatar, opted for complete independence.

Qatar enacted a Provisional Constitution in April 1970, asserting its full statehood for the first time. This declared Qatar an independent Arab state, with its religion Islam, Islamic Sharia as the main source of law, Arabic as the official language and its system of government democratic. A formal declaration of independence was made on September 3rd 1971. On February 22nd of the following year, Sheikh Khalifa assumed power as Emir of the independent State.

RELIGION

Islam is the religion of Qatar, and has been fundamental to the country's way of life since the call to Islam was received. The inhabitants of the Gulf area were quick to embrace the faith, and active in the early Muslim conquests which spread Islam to a wider area.

Many of the mosques to be seen in the older parts of Doha and in the villages are of a traditional style unchanged for centuries. These are now being joined by new mosques of impressive design – such as the Abu Bakr al Siddiq and Omar bin al Khattab mosques in Doha, and the new Wakrah mosque – vivid evidence of the continuing vitality of Islam and the strict adherence to its precepts of the people. Government and Koranic schools alike teach the faith to the nation's young.

Though long unused, the old pearling boats can still be seen on special occasions in Doha bay (above). *Traditional instruments of the pearling trade: weighing the pearls* (far right), *and sieving and grading by size* (right). *An ornate pearl trader's chest* (below right), *in the National Museum.*

Pearling

Until the discovery of oil, the pearling industry was, for Qatar as for most of the Gulf countries, the mainstay of the economy.

The clear, shallow waters and fine sand beds of the Gulf provided an ideal habitat for oysters, which existed in sufficient numbers to support many communities of pearl fishers along the coasts of Qatar. For the duration of the season (from May to September) the entire male population would put to sea, in fleets, with around sixteen men to a boat. On board, the duties of the divers and haulers (*al-seeb*) were precisely defined and regulated by the captain (*nokhada*), and performed often to the accompaniment of chanting and clapping.

The most arduous task fell to the divers. They would descend to the sea bed (usually five to eight fathoms deep), staying underwater for up to a minute before tugging on the ropes to be hauled promptly up to the surface. They would repeat this rigorous performance, exposing themselves to poisonous fish and man-eating sharks, up to fifty times between dawn and dusk. The day's haul would be opened by the entire company, and the pearls extracted and divided according to size and quality.

The pearls found their way, via the pearl merchants (*tawwash*), on to the international market through Baghdad or Bombay. The trade was dealt a double blow in the 1920s and 1930s, by the general depression in world markets which led to the financial crash of 1929, and by competition from the Japanese cultured pearl. Happily for Qatar, the discovery of oil soon after saved the economy from collapse – and men whose ancestors had plied the waters of the Gulf found work on the oilfields, in construction and other sectors of the expanding economy.

The life of the pearler had been one of hardship and scant reward; yet even now, years after the last pearling expedition, those old enough to remember look back on it with nostalgia, and memories of the days of pearling live on in the country's folklore.

Islamic jurisprudence, the Sharia, is the main source of legislation. The Presidency of Sharia Courts and Religious Affairs is responsible for the handling of all religious affairs and the upholding of Islamic values.

GOVERNMENT

The Provisional Constitution decrees that the Emir is the Head of State and holds executive and legislative authority. He issues legislation based on the advice of the Council of Ministers and heads the Council, directs the Ministers' activity and oversees the coordination of Ministries and other Government establishments.

The Council of Ministers is responsible for proposing draft laws and decrees, for implementing these laws and for supervising the financial and administrative affairs of Government.

The present Government consists of fifteen Ministries: Defence, Education, Foreign Affairs, Economy and Trade, Justice, Electricity and Water, Industry and Agriculture, Municipal Affairs, Interior, Finance and Petroleum, Public Works, Labour and Social Affairs, Transport and Communications, Public Health, and Information.

The Advisory Council was established on April 23rd, 1972, to assist the Emir and the Council of Ministers, debating public policy and drafting laws and the budget. Its thirty members represent all sectors of Qatari society.

The judiciary is independent, in both its religious and civil branches, exercising the authority vested in it by the country's constitution.

The armed forces are responsible for the defence of the nation; the Army, the Air Force and the Navy have achieved a high degree of skill and training, and have acquired the latest military technology. The Police are responsible for internal security.

Foreign Affairs

Qatar can still be considered a 'young' state – but, benefiting from a strong and stable leadership, a prosperous economy and a well developed infrastructure, it plays a confident role in regional and world affairs.

Qatar derives further support and a strong sense of unity with its Gulf neighbours from its membership of the Co-operation Council for the Arab States of the Gulf (CCASG). The Council, formed in 1981, of six member states (Saudi Arabia, the United Arab Emirates, Kuwait, Bahrain, Oman and Qatar) has contributed greatly to regional stability and prosperity, and its members have formulated a coordinated stance in international affairs.

Security cooperation agreements back each state's individual defence systems, and joint manoeuvres have been carried out, indications of the region's determination to safeguard its own independence.

Political and economic links are also being strengthened among member states to achieve integration in different fields. One of the Council's most important acts was the

The al Thani

The al Thani family take their name from the family founder, Sheikh Thani bin Mohammad. The family are a branch of the Bani Tamim, one of the oldest tribal confederations on the Arabian mainland, and direct descendants of Mudar bin Nazar. They migrated to Qatar in the eighteenth century. On the death of Sheikh Thani bin Mohammad, the succession passed to his son Sheikh Mohammad, and then to Sheikh Qassim, whose reign spanned an eventful period. Sheikh Qassim's firmness and strength of character were significant in shaping Qatari society and defining its personality – giving it a distinctiveness that put Qatar on the path to independent statehood.

In 1919, Sheikh Abdullah assumed responsibility for the affairs of the emirate. Oil was found in the Dukhan field on the west coast during this reign.

A photograph from the National Museum, of former Rulers (from right to left): *Sheikh Abdullah bin Qassim al Thani, his elder son Sheikh Ali, and his second son Sheikh Hamad, father of the present Emir.*

During his lifetime, Sheikh Abdullah passed authority on to his son Sheikh Hamad, a popular leader, well respected for his faith, ability and breadth of vision. Sheikh Hamed died in 1947, while his son Sheikh Khalifa (the present Emir) was still being prepared to succeed him, so Sheikh Abdullah, though by then advanced in years, again assumed authority. On his death in 1949, as Sheikh Khalifa was still young, the leaders of the al Thani family decided that his uncle, Sheikh Ali should assume power, with Sheikh Khalifa as Heir Apparent. However, Sheikh Ali abdicated in favour of his son Sheikh Ahmad in 1960, when the ruling family again endorsed Sheikh Khalifa as Heir Apparent and Deputy Ruler. It was Sheikh Khalifa who undertook the effective administration of the country.

Sheikh Khalifa announced the end of treaty relations with Britain on September 1st, 1971, thus cancelling the treaty Sheikh Abdullah had signed in 1916.

On September 3rd the independence agreement was signed and Qatar became an independent sovereign state.

On February 22nd, 1972, His Highness Sheikh Khalifa bin Hamad al Thani formally assumed power from his cousin, endorsed by the ruling family, the Qatari people and the armed forces. A new era in Qatar's history was dawning.

On May 31st, 1977, the Emir issued a decree appointing HH Major General Sheikh Hamad bin Khalifa al Thani Heir Apparent and Minister of Defence, in addition to his post as Commander in Chief of the Armed Forces.

---

adoption of the Unified Economic Agreement to encourage freedom of movement between the six members, to pool resources, skills and facilities, and to prevent duplication of economic projects. Specialist organisations have been set up to facilitate joint action, especially in the fields of industry, education, health, sports and media.

Qatar's foreign policy aims to strengthen brotherly relations among Arab and Islamic states, and to defend Arab causes and interests around the world. Qatar, in common with other Arab states which are members of the Arab League, has stressed the need for peace and stability in the region. Since the outbreak of the war between Iraq and Iran in 1980 Qatar has constantly voiced warnings of its threat to regional stability and the world economy. With its Council colleagues it has sought through mediation to end the war.

Qatar has firmly backed the Palestinian cause and has worked with other Arab League members to negotiate a solution that ensures the Palestinians' legitimate rights.

The country upholds the aims and objectives of the United Nations. Qatar maintains twenty-eight diplomatic missions abroad, in all Arab and Islamic States, and most major capital cities. The Emir has enhanced the country's international profile by extensive tours abroad, and also by receiving many foreign Heads of State in Doha. Not least in securing for Qatar an international voice is the country's outstanding record of foreign aid – at times it has contributed as much as seven and a half per cent of its annual oil revenue. The country has for long stressed its commitment to aid for other developing countries.

THE ECONOMY

Development

Following independence, with oil production under state control, Qatar turned to the question of its long term economic development. The most pressing concern was the country's total dependence on crude oil exports for revenue. Oil reserves were known to be finite, and esimates at the time suggested (in fact pessimistically) that they would run out within two decades. An urgent need was recognised to diversify the economy – yet the country possessed few natural resources, little cultivable land and a climate little suited to agriculture.

Qatar opted, therefore, for extensive investment in capital-intensive industries, which could take advantage of the country's hydrocarbon reserves and maximise recovery of these resources. Before independence, Qatar's experience of heavy industry had been limited, though the Qatar National Cement Company had been set up in Umm Bab in 1965.

A Gas Liquids complex, petrochemicals and fertiliser industries and a large steel plant were established in the newly designated heavy industrial zone at Umm Said during the 1970s, with Government finance and the participation of specialist foreign companies. Now the Government actively encourages private enterprise through its Industrial Development Technical Centre (IDTC), which offers soft loans for approved projects, and low rents on the Salwa Road light industrial estate outside Doha. Many of the new manufacturing projects which have been granted licences are already in operation there; the busy estate is a visible sign of the success of the Government's initiative.

In order that the Qataris could become involved in developing the country and managing its resources, a long term policy was required, involving extensive training and incentive schemes. The Government is concerned that qualified Qataris should play an active role in the running of the economy, and that nationals should be encouraged to invest at home rather than abroad.

In most respects, Government policies appear to bring steady success. Exports, until 1970 consisting entirely of crude oil, have since diversified: by 1982 non-hydrocarbon exports contributed ten per cent of the total, and the country was using its own reserves to fuel and supply local secondary industries. New economic sectors are growing, and local banking facilities have expanded. The country's financial affairs are directed by the Qatar Monetary Agency, the central bank authority, from its headquarters in Doha. Fifteen banks are operating in the capital, five of them

Qatari. There has been a sharp rise in the number of Qataris at high levels in finance, commerce and industry.

While striving to expand its economic base and to achieve self-sufficiency, Qatar continues to pursue a policy of economic cooperation with other member states of the CCASG.

In common with other large oil producers, Qatar's economy has been affected by declining world markets for oil and resulting strict production quotas. Some adjustment in public spending levels has proved necessary at times, but judicious long term planning and rationalised public spending have minimised the effects on economic development. Qatar's economic future has been assured to a large extent even after the eventual depletion of its oil resources by the discovery of vast reserves of non-associated natural gas in its offshore territory. Feasibility studies for the exploitation of these reserves envisage full scale production by the 1990s. Already the discovery has had a stimulating effect on the economy, boosting confidence and affecting economic and financial planning.

Petroleum

Oil production remains the backbone of the country's economy, providing around ninety per cent of Qatar's revenue. Since oil was first produced at Dukhan's No. 1 well, in 1949, it has profoundly influenced the rate and character of the country's economic development.

Qatar's onshore deposits, accounting for half the level of production, lie in four hydrocarbon reservoirs in a narrow field running along the west coast, below the low limestone ridge known as the 'Dukhan Heights'. Offshore reserves lie in four fields around Halul Island, to the east of the country: Id al-Shargi, Maydan Mahzam, Bul Hanine and Al Bunduq, the last shared equally with Abu Dhabi.

The state-owned Qatar General Petroleum Corporation (QGPC) took over onshore operations from the Qatar Petroleum Company in 1976, and offshore operations from the Shell Company of Qatar the following year.

The bulk of oil exports go to Japan and other Far Eastern countries. Production reached a peak of 570,000 barrels per day in 1973; after this, quotas reduced output in the face of declining world markets. QGPC's emphasis now is more than ever on maximising recovery rather than production, and reducing production costs – by the utilisation of associated gas, and the elimination of wasteful flaring – and in the refining of its own crude oil. QGPC's expansion in the 1980s is geared mostly towards its downstream industries and oil refining: it is the major shareholder in the country's fertiliser and petrochemicals industries. The Corporation supplies natural gas to the Umm Said NGL plant; its new refinery at Umm Said, in operation since 1983, satisfies all local needs for refined products and has begun to export its surplus.

QGPC's current policies reflect its clear vision of its direction for the future.

Gas

QGPC's policy of 'optimum recovery', and its plans to utilise the associated gas from its own oilfields began in 1971, with proposals for a Natural Gas Liquids (NGL) complex at Umm Said, which now houses two plants. One processes gas liquids from onshore oilfields, producing natural gas liquids and petrochemical feedstock (ethane-rich gas, propane, butane and condensate); the other utilises gas and gas liquids from offshore in the production of natural gas liquids, petrochemical feedstock and industrial fuel gas. Now, nearly all associated gas from onshore, and an increasing proportion from offshore, is put to use. The complex provides a vital energy source for local factories and power stations, as well as feedstock for the nearby petrochemicals industry and reducing agent for local steel production. The surplus goes for export direct from the company's own jetty at Umm Said.

Of greater significance for the future is the 'North Field' reservoir of non-associated gas from the 'khuff' formation discovered in Qatari territorial waters in the early seventies. The field, covering 6000 square kilometres, is estimated to be the world's largest single gas reservoir.

The scale of investment and preparation necessary to develop this field is vast; it is the most important single undertaking in Qatar for decades, and has called for extensive planning. The North Field Steering Committee, formed by the Emir in November 1984, envisages a three-stage

The new QGPC oil refinery at Umm Said.

development, leading to the eventual construction of a new liquid natural gas plant at Umm Said, and export of the gas throughout the world. The first stage – design, procurement, construction and installation of equipment and structures and a pipeline link to Umm Said – was expected to be complete by 1988, although production will not significantly affect Qatar's export figures for some time after that. The immense capital investment needed for this development is likely to bring in other member states of the CCASG during phase two of the development – but plans depend on the level of world demand into the 1990s.

Heavy Industry

The Qatar Fertiliser Company was the first enterprise to arrive at the Umm Said heavy industrial zone. It was established in 1969 in cooperation with Norsk Hydro and other experts in the field, and began production in 1973.

The plant uses natural gas piped from Dukhan, sea water and air to make liquid ammonia, the base material of the fertiliser industry. New plants were commissioned in 1976, designed to double production capacity of ammonia and urea. The bulk of these products is exported, from the company's jetty, mainly to India and China.

In 1978, some kilometres further north, the Qatar Steel Company began operation. Though the basic material, raw iron pellets, had to be imported (from Sweden and Brazil) to supply the direct reduction plant, QASCO was able to make use of natural gas from the 'khuff' formation under Dukhan's oilfields, and water and electricity from the new power station at Ras Abu Fontas. Molten steel is produced from sponge iron and scrap in an electric arc furnace, and cast into billets. Reinforcing steel bars are produced and exported, chiefly to neighbouring Gulf states.

In 1981 Qatar and Saudi Arabia signed an agreement to cooperate on buying, marketing and training policies – an example of the economic strategy encouraged by the CCASG. Although the company has recently been affected by falling world prices for steel, it is regarded by the World Bank as a 'model project'. In line with the policy to encourage participation by Qataris, the transfer to local management is already well advanced.

The Qatar Petrochemical Company was founded in 1974, with support from the French petrochemicals firm CdF Chimie. It set up next to QAFCO at Umm Said, coming on stream in 1980. The plant makes use of ethane-rich gas, supplied by the nearby NGL plant, to produce high quality ethylene and low-density polyethylene, with sulphur as a by-product. It is the largest such plant in the Arab region, with 650 employees, and supplies neighbouring countries as well as fulfilling local demand. A new ethylene plant has been designed to raise ethylene production significantly from its present level. QAPCO is now a partner with the French petrochemical company Copenor, which has a holding of forty per cent.

Agriculture

Qatar has long sought to increase agricultural production, with the aim of self-sufficiency by the year 2000. It is widely believed now that this objective may be too optimistic. Only three per cent of Qatar's territory is at present cultivable; there is the continuing problem of harsh climate, shortage and expense of irrigation water, soil infertility, and a certain reluctance among nationals to engage in agriculture as a commercial enterprise.

Despite these problems, there are over seven hundred farms in the country, and the number is on the increase. Many, though not all, are run as commercial concerns, and with large-scale Government investment in agricultural technology, production too is rising in all sectors.

The most striking progress has been made in vegetable production, which does meet local demand in winter, and most summer requirements. In controlled conditions most varieties of vegetable can now be grown.

All this has required large-scale public and private investment. Through the Industrial Development Technical Centre, experimental farming projects have led to greater cultivation and soil fertility. Greenhouse projects have been widely introduced, and there has been research into the purification of brackish water by solar powered reverse osmosis, and the cultivation of crops and sand, using solar

Dhows at Wakrah.

Doha in the 1960s (top) *Looking from the al Khleifat district in the South Bay, towards the port and the town centre; the former Royal Palace, now restored as the Qatar National Museum, is in the centre. The al Hitmi district* (left), *with the Royal Palace complex top right, against the sea.*

power and sea water – attempts to reduce the demands of agriculture on expensive desalination processes.

Livestock projects, too, have been implemented: cattle, sheep and poultry are now reared in farms around the country, and much animal fodder is grown locally. Small scale factories have been set up to process and market dairy produce. The fishing industry, centred on Doha, Al Khor and Wakrah, continues to expand.

Complete agricultural self-sufficiency may not be attainable, but a healthy and growing agricultural industry has been developed, and it is Government policy to ensure that this rapid growth continues.

Construction

Large scale construction accompanied the growth of the country's infrastructure in the 1950s and 1960s, with the building of industrial sites, power and desalination plants

and roads. The Popular Housing Scheme, inaugurated in 1964 with the aim of providing Qataris with their own modern home, brought a surge of residential development.

The increase in oil revenue in the 1970s brought the acceleration and the completion of most infrastructural projects, a modern road network, and massive housing developments throughout the country, with Doha itself an enormous building site, expanding daily. This construction boom probably passed its peak in the early 1980s, and the industry has slackened off since; but major long term projects will continue, mostly in the capital and the industrial centre of Umm Said.

Activity in Doha is centred on the 'New District of Doha' in the West Bay – begun in 1974 and expected to continue until the turn of the century. This vast extension of the capital will accommodate a third of Doha's growth over this period, and allow the city room to 'breathe'. Much of it is on

Approaching Doha from the sea (above). *The dhow harbour and central square of Doha* (right). *Most of the surrounding buildings have since been replaced, but the clock tower, seen here under construction in the middle of the square, still stands.*

land reclaimed from the sea, in an extension of the crescent shape of Doha Bay.

Following a detailed masterplan, the district has been mapped out around focal points and centres of activity: the Corniche, which provides a link with the city centre; zones for government ministries, for commercial headquarters and diplomatic missions; and residential communities, each with its own centre of local services. To the north lies the new campus of Qatar University, and land designated for a large National Park.

Building in the area is carefully monitored, and must conform to the highest standards of design. The character of the district is already evident.

In Umm Said, continuing construction has brought new life to the industrial zone. Large scale residential areas house much of the factories' work force, and shops, banks, sports and entertainment centres are being provided to create a town independent of the capital.

Construction sites, new roads, schools, factories, mosques and villas appear everywhere. Soon, the Al Wusail desalination plant and power station complex, and offshore construction for the North Field gas industry, will lead to more large-scale construction programmes.

Communications

The country now has an efficient network of internal communications and advanced links with the outside world.

Modern roads connect every settlement, and enable goods to be transported overland from Qatar's industrial zones, linking factories with the capital and the ports. Fast trunk roads connect Qatar with the neighbouring states of Saudi Arabia and the United Arab Emirates. The four ring roads around Doha have done much to ease access to the interior and relieve congestion in the city centre.

With the coming of oil and heavy industry there was an urgent need for a deep water port in the country, to replace the small and shallow fishing harbours of the previous era. A broad trench was cut through the reef blocking Doha's natural harbour in 1963, and port facilities there handle most of Qatar's cargo traffic. After extensive surveys, however, deep water access to the shoreline was finally found at Umm Said, and a port established which takes all the country's large-scale shipping. Oil exports are loaded from terminals here, and the heavy industrial zone was set up within easy reach. The Government is conducting feasibility studies for access channels to new ports to cope with the further increase in shipping.

Qatar has a quarter share (with Bahrain, the UAE and Oman) in Gulf Air, the national carrier. Doha International Airport, on the southern edge of the city, copes with ever more air traffic, as Gulf Air's network of international flights expands. Proposals are being considered for an extra runway, or even for the construction of a new airport outside Doha.

Qatar's telecommunications system is equally advanced. The telephone network now covers nearly all the country,

Minaret overlooking Doha harbour (right). *The entrance to the Qatar National Museum* (far right).

and international calls can be made by satellite, cable and microwave. Two earth stations at Mukheinis, in central Qatar, linked to Intelsat's satellites over the Indian and Atlantic Oceans, provide excellent connections to most points of the globe. A submarine cable connection to Bahrain and the UAE was opened recently, and this is to be extended to other Gulf states. Plans are now going ahead for the construction of a ground station to link with the Arabian Satellite Communication Organisation's Arabsat network.

THE PEOPLE

Culture and Heritage

Among the office blocks, houses and new towns of modern Qatar, the remaining traditional buildings provide a vivid reminder of Qatar before the oil era. The merchants' houses of Wakrah and Doha, with their imposing wind towers, the fortified turrets of a stronghold in Umm Salal Mohammad, the fort at Zubara, old mosques at Wakrah and Ruwais – all these reflect a way of life unique to the region and unchanged for centuries, shaped by the climate, the routines and occupations of daily life and the social structure of old Qatar.

The Qatar National Museum, opened in the 1970s, is housed in the old palace complex in Doha, the residence of the Al Thani family until the 1930s. The beautifully restored buildings are fine examples of the Qatari style, using available materials, fitted to the climate and the daily needs of social life. The Qataris built light structures, of stone, coral and mortar, with ceilings of mangrove poles and woven reeds. The beauty of these buildings lies in their simplicity: walls were decorated with restrained, delicate gypsum carvings, and simple air vents in the walls, or the distinctive wind towers, provided effective natural ventilation.

All houses, great or small, were constructed on similar lines. Nearly all lay along the shoreline, close to the harbours, and within reach of the light sea breezes. The inhabitants lived the life of the sea, which has strongly influenced and enriched Qatar's cultural heritage.

The exhibits at the Qatar National Museum illustrate this unique lifestyle, between the traditions of the desert and the maritime influence of settlements in the Gulf, Asia and East Africa. Qatari craftsmen are renowned for their intricate and detailed embroidery and fabric weaving – striking examples of embroidered *thaubs* and *abbas* are on display at the Museum beside the woven and dyed textiles of the Bedouin. Jewellery, too, has always flourished, using local Gulf pearls as well as the gold and silver imported to make the wide variety of bracelets, necklaces and headdresses which adorned Qatari brides.

Of necessity, the Qataris were skilled boatbuilders. Their finely crafted dhows can still be seen: the *boum*, the *jalbout*, the *sho'a* and the *sambuq*, the traditional pearling vessel, now motorised and still used for fishing. Attempts are being made to revive these ancient skills in boatyards along the Corniche.

For a people who knew few luxuries it is not surprising that – as with the Bedouin – their traditional culture is most strongly expressed in their folklore and music rather than in artefacts. The Bedouin inheritance itself is clearest in the noble arts of poetry and oration – whether in the classical Arabic style or in the more colloquial *nabati* verse, often composed in local dialect, traditional modes have given much to recent Qatari writing.

Music and singing, which provided the only respite from the monotony of long pearling expeditions, is also a living part of their heritage. A rich variety of folk songs dwells on the joys, sorrows, customs and traditions of life by the sea. Musical instruments show an affinity with those of East Africa: pipes, tambourines, drums, stringed instruments and flutes. The formal, stately dances which their music accompanied are still performed today – at national festivals, and on social occasions, at religious feasts and weddings.

So much of this tradition is oral folklore, in danger of being lost in the rapid pace of development. The Qataris recognised this threat, and have worked to record and preserve this precious lore for future generations.

The country is determined to preserve what is valuable of its heritage and tradition; it holds strongly to these traditions, recognising in them a vital expression of their small country's distinct identity.

Health

The Government provides free comprehensive health services to all, nationals and expatriates alike. An all-embracing programme of development, seen as a high priority, has brought a medical registration scheme to all inhabitants, primary health care and medical centres to every settlement, and far-reaching preventive medicine and health education programmes. Environmental health is an important issue, and advanced regulations have been brought in regarding safety conditions at work. Voluntary societies like the Qatar Red Crescent run frequent public health campaigns around the capital and in the media.

Such is the pace of development that hospitals built in the 1960s have already been modernised, and better equipped hospitals have been built beside them. Demand has increased for specialist medical and surgical treatment hitherto only available abroad. The Hamad General Hospital in central Doha, opened in 1982, boasts the most advanced medical equipment and services, and is regarded as one of the foremost hospitals in the Gulf area. Specialist facilities there include cardio-vascular surgery, a plastic surgery unit, computerised tomography for the diagnosis of head injuries, and the advanced Nuclear Medicine section, the first of its kind in the Gulf. A large new maternity hospital adjoins the Hamad General Hospital, and the Rumailah Hospital, previously the country's largest, is being transformed into a specialist centre for geriatrics and the handicapped.

More Qataris are becoming involved in the health service, especially at a senior administrative level. Extensive in-service training programmes have been provided to encourage this trend. The Hamad General Hospital has become a postgraduate training centre for Qataris who have graduated from Arab medical schools; and many are sent abroad for higher studies in hospital administration.

Education

Before 1952, the only schools in Qatar were the religious institutes, or *kuttab*, where the Koran was taught and memorised. It was recognised from the start that much of the country's progress depended on the rapid development of a full educational system, and the Ministry of Education was the first Ministry to be established. A primary system began in 1956, and as the first years of schoolchildren advanced, higher levels of education were introduced: intermediate in 1958, and secondary in the early 1960s. The system was completed, in 1973, by the foundation of the Higher Teacher Training College, the nucleus of the new University of Qatar.

Pupils specialise from secondary level, following either scientific, literary, religious, technical or commercial disciplines. Previously reliant on teachers from other Arab countries, Qatar's educational system has now come of age, as a number of the first generation of Qatari school children have risen through it to become teachers themselves.

A major landmark in Qatari education was the foundation of the University in 1977. The campus then envisaged is now finished, and open to students – an enormous, highly ac-

The younger generation.

claimed architectural complex of interlocking cells housing the different faculties, with a dominant motif of traditional Qatari wind towers.

The six faculties – Education, Science, Humanities and Social Sciences, Sharia and Islamic Studies, Engineering, and Business Administration and Economy – have the most up-to-date equipment, laboratories and lecture halls. Specialist centres have been set up for scientific, technical and educational research.

The needs of industry and commerce are also considered highly important by the Government, and specialist instruction, to international standards, is organised by the Training and Career Development Department. At the Vocational Training Centre in Doha, Qataris can equip themselves with the practical and technical skills required by the many new State industries and private enterprises.

Facilities at every level continue to improve and expand with Qatar's rising population. A ten-year programme of school-building has seen the completion of sixty fully-equipped schools in Doha and outside; the system which in 1954 provided instruction for five hundred students now caters for forty thousand.

Recreation

Modern life has brought more free time for all; it has also provided more opportunities and activities to pursue. The desert exerts a continuing attraction for many at weekends, and the ancient arts of falconry and camel racing are still pursued in season. Today's crowds, however, are drawn just as much to the city's new parks, the racecourse at Rayyan, the beaches at Doha and outside the city, and the marinas around Doha Bay. At weekends the bay is dotted with multi-coloured sails, motorboats and waterskiers, providing an endless source of interest for the crowds which gather along the Corniche, to fish, walk or meet friends. The new Zoo, outside the city, is a popular spot for outings – an oasis of greenery, fountains and ponds providing a controlled environment for a large number of animals. Travel abroad has become popular also, especially in the hot summer months, when many Qataris holiday elsewhere in the Middle East, in Europe, America or the Far East.

The Government has provided excellent facilities to cater for the explosion of interest in sports of all kinds. Under the supervision of the Supreme Council for Youth Welfare financial support has been given for a growing number of sports and youth clubs around the country, with provisions for soccer, athletics, swimming, basketball, and volleyball among others. Frequent sporting events and league matches are held, and are well attended.

Soccer has without doubt become the national sport. At international matches, crowds pack the Khalifa Olympic Stadium (part of the national Sports City in Rayyan) which seats forty thousand. A Qatar National Olympic Committee has been set up to encourage and support athletes' participation in world sporting events, and has already had striking successes, so soon after Qatar's entry into this larger arena. The national soccer team's performance at home and abroad has at times defied all predictions – as when they qualified for the Los Angeles Olympic Games in 1984, earning themselves a chance to play against the world's best. With growing experience, continuing enthusiasm and the best facilities, their standing in international competitions can only improve.

The people of Qatar, in a few decades, have lived through changes which elsewhere in the world have taken centuries to achieve. The older generation, fishermen or desert dwellers in their youth, have seen their children engage in the technicalities of oil production and international banking, medicine and science; they have moved into fully equipped modern homes, and enjoy all the benefits of modern life. Such changes have not always been easy to absorb, and some still look back with nostalgia on the harder life of the past, regarding with caution modern ways and the problems they bring. This caution may well be a strength, a check against the dangers and turmoil of over-rapid development.

Qatar, despite its small size and population and its relative youth, is a nation with a clear vision of its position within the Arab world and beyond, and is fully conscious of its role in international affairs. It is a nation confidently on the advance; yet it values its heritage and traditions and will not jeopardise its own strengths and identity in a headlong rush of development.

THE LAND

Fishermen's dhows off the east coast; net mending in Doha dhow harbour.

Dusk at Wakrah dhow harbour.
(*overleaf*) Dawn return for
fishermen at Al Khor.

Eroded rock formations on the north east coast near Fuwairat (*left*).
The fishermen of the coastal villages have moved to new towns with modern facilities; only the abandoned houses remain as a reminder of former, harder, times.

Preceding pages: Qatar's varied terrain: coastal swamps near Al Khor *(top)*; salt flats, or *sabkha (middle)* and dunes at Khor al Udeid, the 'inland sea' on the country's southern border *(bottom and right)*.

These pages: Eroded limestone formations in the desert near Dukhan *(right)*; dawn in the desert near Khor al Udeid *(left)*. A herd of rheem in a private park at Ras Ushairij in the north west *(above)*. The rare Arabian Oryx has been reared successfully for decades at Shahaniyah National Park, in central Qatar *(above left)*.

At Umm Salal Mohammad: an old man
of the village; the towers and
crenellations of a fortified house in
traditional Qatari style; date plantations
have long existed around the country's
natural wells.

Outside Doha, some traditional activities survive: camels reared near the Saudi border *(left)*; livestock raising in the north *(below)*.

The ruined city of Zubara, in the north-west, which flourished in the late 18th century, has recently been excavated and preserved (*above and above right*). (*right and far right*) At the old mosque on the waterfront at Ruwais.

Preceding pages: The entrance to Doha Fort, built in the last century and now fully restored for its new role as a museum. *These pages:* The National Museum of Qatar: the complex, the residence of the al Thani ruling family until the 1930s, has been handsomely restored. It is the finest example of indigenous architecture in the country, and an ideal setting for the Museum.

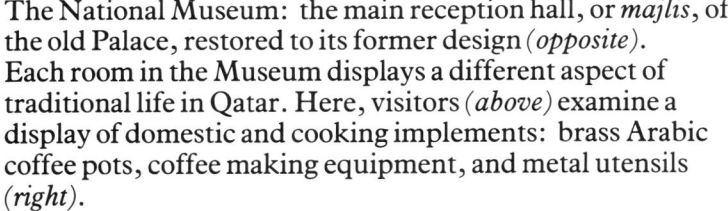

The National Museum: the main reception hall, or *majlis*, of the old Palace, restored to its former design *(opposite)*. Each room in the Museum displays a different aspect of traditional life in Qatar. Here, visitors *(above)* examine a display of domestic and cooking implements: brass Arabic coffee pots, coffee making equipment, and metal utensils *(right)*.

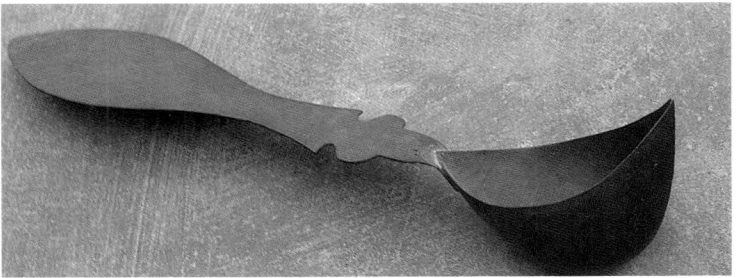

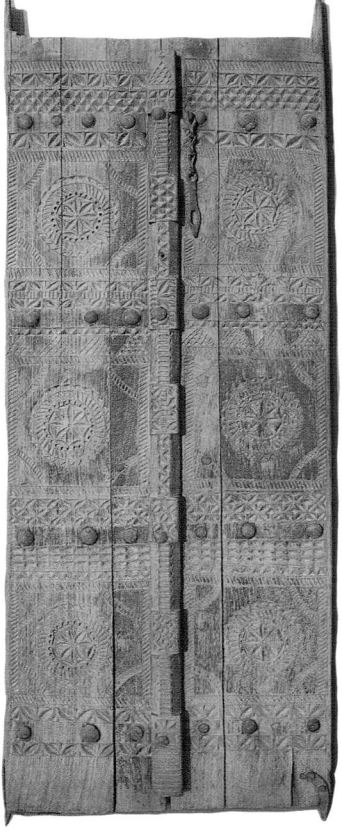

The crafts of Qatari builders can still be seen in the ornately carved doors of the Al Bida district of the old town *(above and right)*, and preserved in the handsome restored ceilings *(middle and bottom centre)* and carved wall decorations *(top centre and far right)* of the National Museum; decoration of the New Emiri Palace of Doha has provided an opportunity to continue this skilled handcarving *(above right)*.

Qataris, of necessity, have always been experienced boatbuilders. The lagoon of the National Museum (*top left*) houses examples of many different types of local craft, from the large ocean-going *boum* (*above, and detail, left*) to the simple *shashah*, made of date palm sticks bound with *coir* and formerly used for inshore fishing (*far left*).

The *sambuq*, a traditional fishing vessel, has been motorised and many are still seen working from Doha harbour (*bottom centre*).

The Qatar National Museum provides an important record of the fast-disappearing lifestyle and crafts of the Bedouin. A goat-hair Bedouin tent *(above left)*, the Museum's central exhibit; a fringed camel saddle bag *(left)*, a fine example of Bedouin weaving. *(far left)* Women and children were usually carried on camels in a riding litter *(maksar)*, of decorated bent wood and leather. The Bedouin tradition of falconry has survived, and is keenly pursued in the desert in season *(above right)*. A *rezeef* dance *(right):* such performances are a highlight at national celebrations.

Friday prayer packs the large new mosque of Abu Bakr al Siddiq in Doha *(left)*. Leaving the new Wakrah mosque after evening prayer *(above)*.

Recent building has broadened the architectural range of Qatar's mosques: the new and highly ornate mosque at Wakrah *(left)* and the Abu Bakr al Siddiq mosque *(below)* have attracted great admiration.

The impressive Omar bin al Khattab mosque in the New District of Doha (*above and below left*); a contrast to the traditional design of the minaret at Fuwairat, in the north (*right*).

GOVERNMENT

The New Emiri Palace (*above*) overlooking the Corniche in the centre of the city is one of Doha's most impressive landmarks and a focal point of the city skyline.

The Emir's weeky *majlis*, or audience, in the Palace (*right*) provides a direct link between the ruler and the people; access is free to all.

Together with the Council of Ministers, the Advisory Council fulfills an important public role as a consultative body. Its thirty members represent all sectors and areas of the country. HH the Emir addressing the Advisory Council *(above);* the Council in session *(right).*

The Government consists of fifteen Ministries, many of which have been recently rehoused in impressive buildings on the Corniche: *(opposite, above)* the Ministry of Finance and petroleum; *(opposite, below)* the Ministry of the Interior.

Various Police departments carry the responsibility for internal security, traffic control, fire prevention, ports and immigration. *(above left)* Traffic police on point duty on the Corniche. At Rayyan Police Training Institute: dog handling *(left)*; the Police Band *(top)*. Fire officers at the new Doha Fire Station *(above)*.

FOREIGN AFFAIRS & DEFENCE

The Ministry of Foreign Affairs (*right*). Qatar hosts a summit conference of the Cooperation Council for the Arab States of the Gulf in Doha (*below*).

(*above*) HH the Emir meeting world Leaders at home and abroad. (*left*) HH the Emir with Heads of CCASG member states.

The Qatari armed forces' Air Arm: Qatari pilots check flight details in the Navigation Room (*below*); a fighter pilot prepares for take-off (*right*); pilots in the cockpit of a Sea King helicopter (*far right*); a Mirage fighter plane on the runway (*below right*).

The Navy: on board a missile frigate *(right)*; the bridge *(opposite)*; action stations on deck *(above)*.

The Emiri Armoured Arm: tank manoeuvres in the desert
(*right and below*); weapons training (*opposite, bottom*).
Commando excercises (*opposite, top*), and the Special
Emergency Force in training (*opposite, middle*).

MODERN LIFE

Preceding pages: On Doha's new Corniche.

These pages: The new Corniche *(top left)* extends round the full sweep of the bay to the Sheraton Hotel. Here, building land is being reclaimed from the sea *(above right)* and new housing contrasts strongly with the adjacent old quarters of Doha *(far right)*. Full facilities, including efficient ring roads and water storage *(right)* have been provided to cope with this expansion.

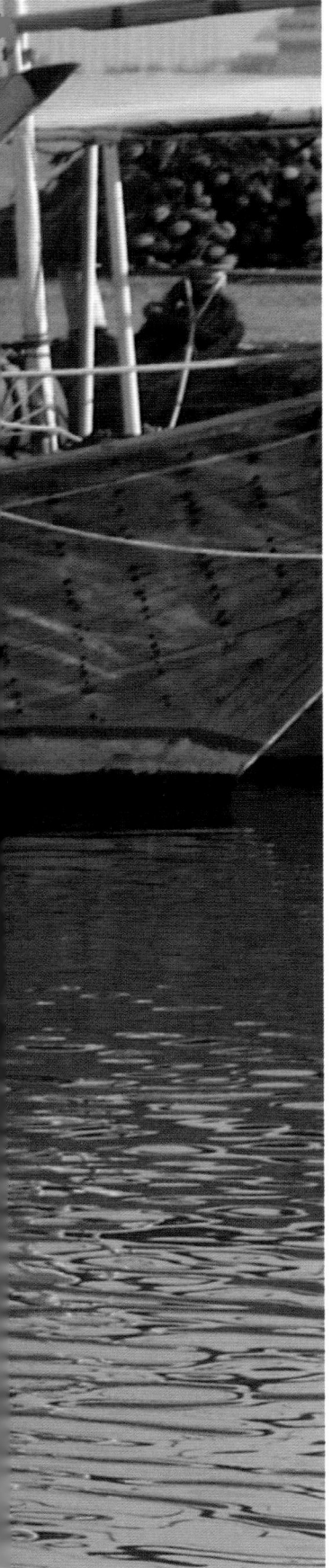

The old dhow harbour on Doha's waterfront is still a focus of great activity at all times of day.
Overleaf: The old ways of life persist within sight of the ultra-modern Sheraton Hotel, seen in stark profile across the bay.

Much of Doha's old souq has been rehoused in a modern complex on the Salwa Road, providing greater space and improved facilities: offloading produce (*far left*); the fish market and fruit and vegetable stalls (*above left*); a young shopper (*above*). However, the original souq in the centre of Doha (*left*) still retains much of its character.

Modern life has brought to Doha hypermarkets (*above*), luxury shops (*below*), and international class hotels; shown here (*right*) is the interior of the Doha Sheraton.

The acclaimed architecture of the Doha Sheraton (*left*); the
Oasis and Gulf hotels in the South Bay area (*top*); the new
Ramada Renaissance hotel (*above*).

The National Theatre *(top and middle right, below)*, opened in 1982, hosts a variety of well-attended performances.
The Television and Broadcasting Centre in Doha *(bottom right and opposite)* has facilities which bring an expanding range of programmes to a wider public.

Qatar Television filming on location in the specially restored 'traditional fishing village' of Al Mafjar, in the north. Series dramatising the old life are becoming increasingly popular.

A traditional Qatari wedding; separate celebrations for
men and women, with music, dancing and food, are open
to all, old and young. The assembly later moves in
procession to the bride's house for the formal ceremony.

The building boom of the last fifteen years has transformed the city, and is still continuing. New residential complexes (*below*) have been built in the New District; along the ring roads, family housing (*bottom*) has provided Qataris with all modern facilities and surrounding gardens. The new Emiri Palace (*left*), a project of enormous proportions and grandeur, is a recent addition to the Doha skyline.

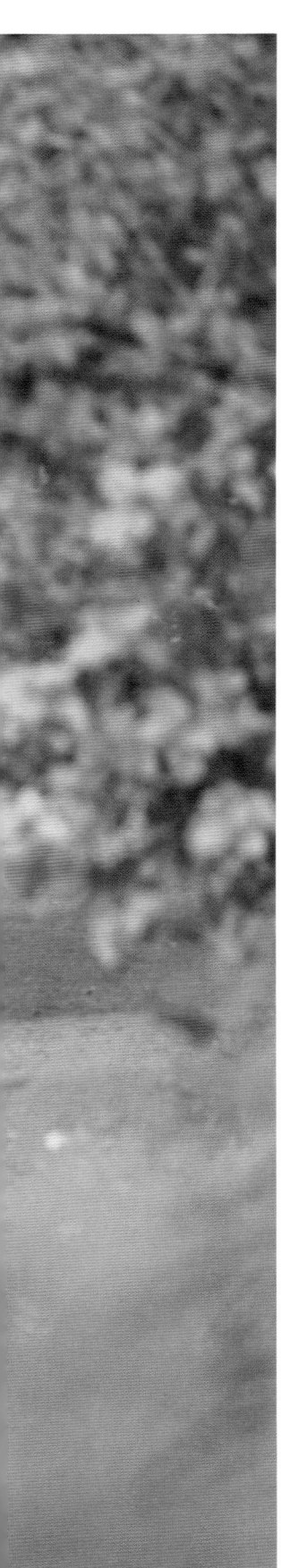

Planners have provided the city with green parks, popular spots at weekends and in the evening with family groups and young children, far from the noise of the urban centre.

QATAR RALLY رالي قطر
START 1985 FINISH

In recent years there has been a surge of interest in many sports – including sailing and motor racing (*above and left*). Fine facilities cater for this interest: the Khalifa Olympic Stadium in Khalifa Sports City (*top left*) holds up to 45,000 spectators for local, national and international sporting events, and the racecourse at Rayyan (*far left*) holds race meetings of Arab thoroughbreds, as well as occasional (less serious) camel races.

New recreations and old: returning to Doha marina at dusk (*left*); a traditional *rezeef* dance (*above*), performed at national celebrations, to the accompaniment of the *lewa* (*right*).

The Doha Zoo, on the Salwa Road outside the city, with its distinctive architecture, lush gardens, pools and fountains, provides a controlled environment for a wide variety of local and exotic animals. It is a stark contrast to the surrounding desert, and a popular destination for evening and weekend outings from the city.

Though a small country and relatively new to the sport, Qatar's performance in international soccer matches has frequently defied all expectations, and resulted in some well-remembered victories. Here, an International match at the Al Arabi Stadium (*right*) calls for considerable ceremony (*below*), and a large crowd (*overleaf*) supports the home team.

INDUSTRY, COMMERCE & AGRICULTURE

Fifty years after oil was first struck in the Dukhan fields, the search still continues. Here, an exploratory drilling rig, north of Dukhan, probes for oil and gas to a possible depth of 18,000 ft.

Oil production: at a well head treatment plant (*above right*); at Khatiya gassing station (*above left*), where the raw intake of oil and gas is separated by a centrifugal process; and Fahahil stripping station (*top, right*) where methane-rich gas is drawn off from the raw natural gas, to supply the state gas distribution system.

Offshore oil operations are centred on Halul Island *(below)*, to the east of Qatar. Nearby are grouped oil rigs and production stations *(right)*.

The Natural Gas Liquids plant at Umm Said processes associated gas from onshore and offshore fields. The control room (*right*) regulates the operations of the two plants and the loading of export tankers; low-temperature propane and butane storage tanks on the shoreline (*above*); one of the complex's two processing plants (*far right*).

116

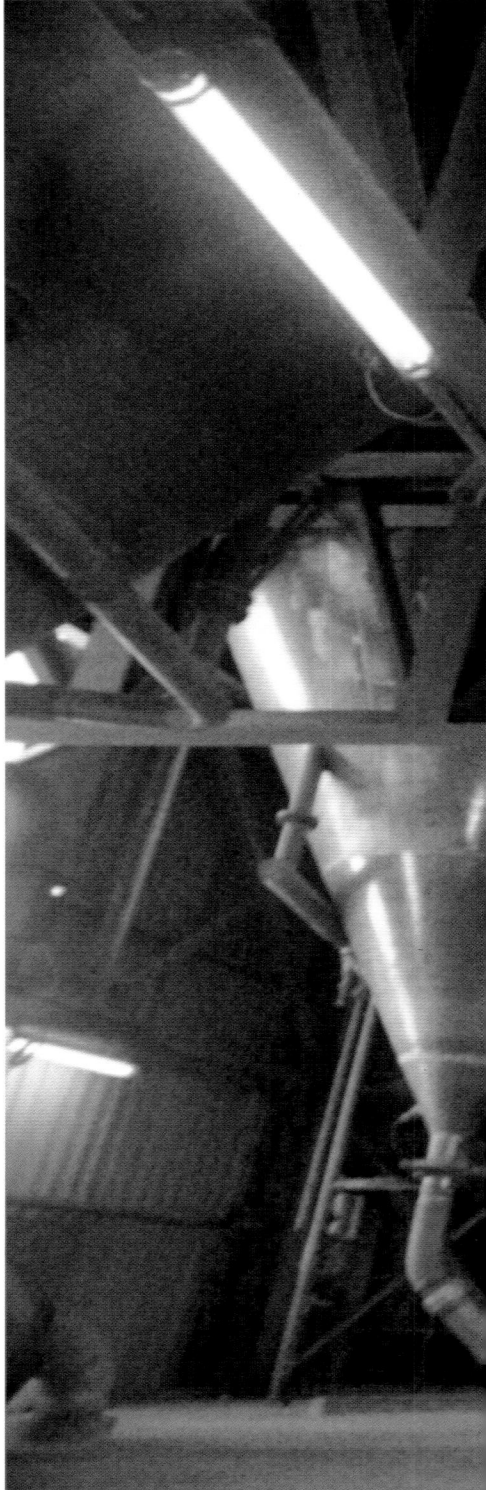

The Qatar Petrochemical Company (QAPCO) complex *(top left)* at Umm Said produces ethylene, polyethylene and sulphur, utilising ethane-rich gas from the nearby Natural Gas liquids complex. Inside the silo unit *(right)*.
(above) The control room of the adjacent Qatar Fertilizer Company (QAFCO).

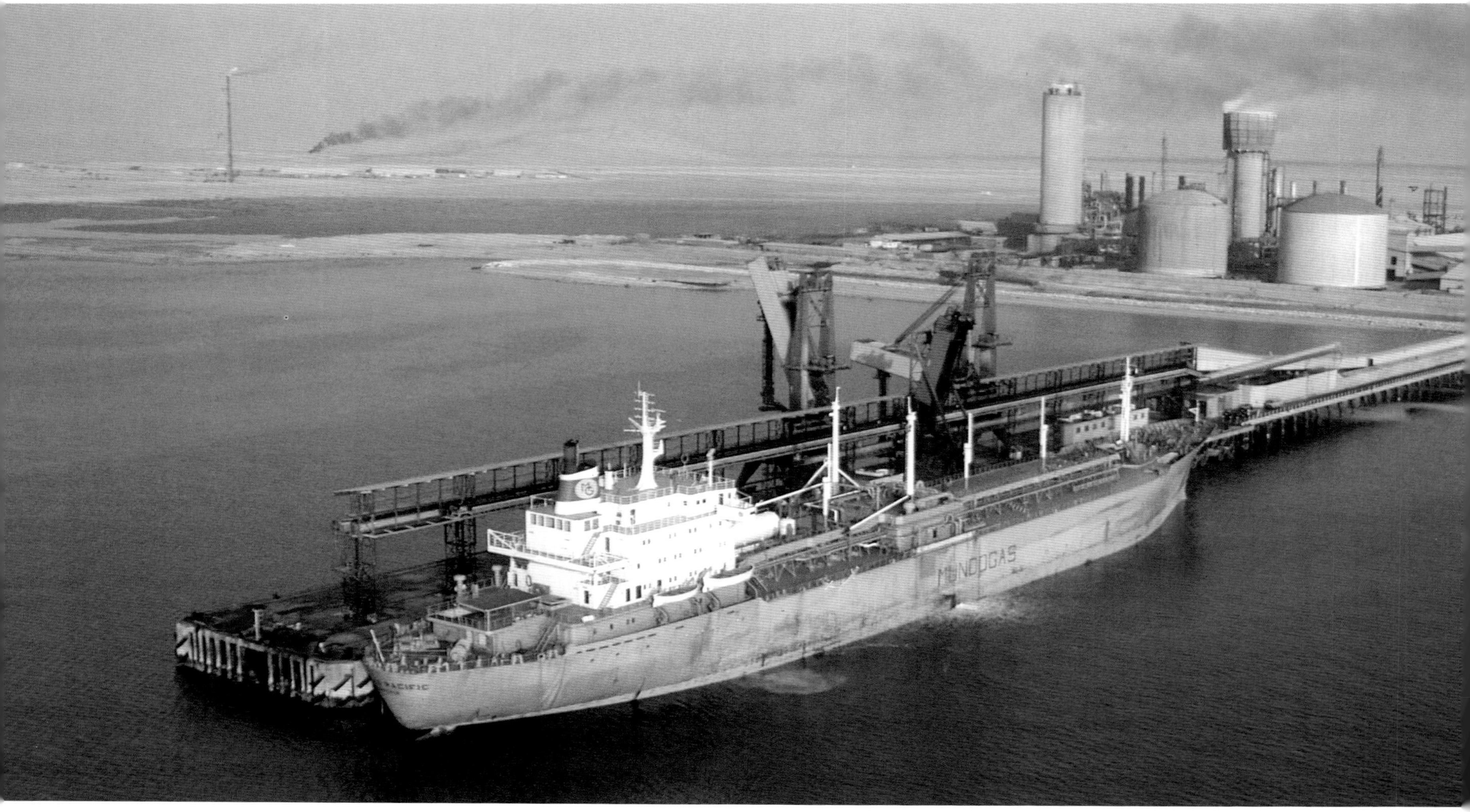
MUNDOGAS

Viking Ship Brand
Norsk Hydro
UREA 46%N
FERTILISER GRADE
50 kilos net
GAFCO
PRODUCED IN QATAR BY
QATAR FERTILISER COMPANY
USE NO HOOKS

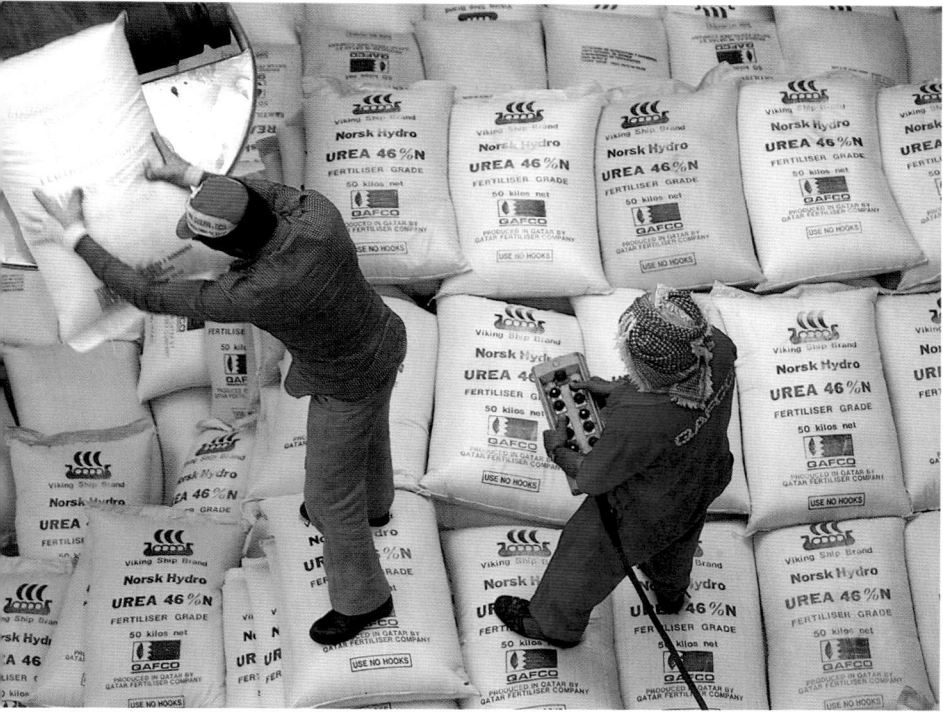

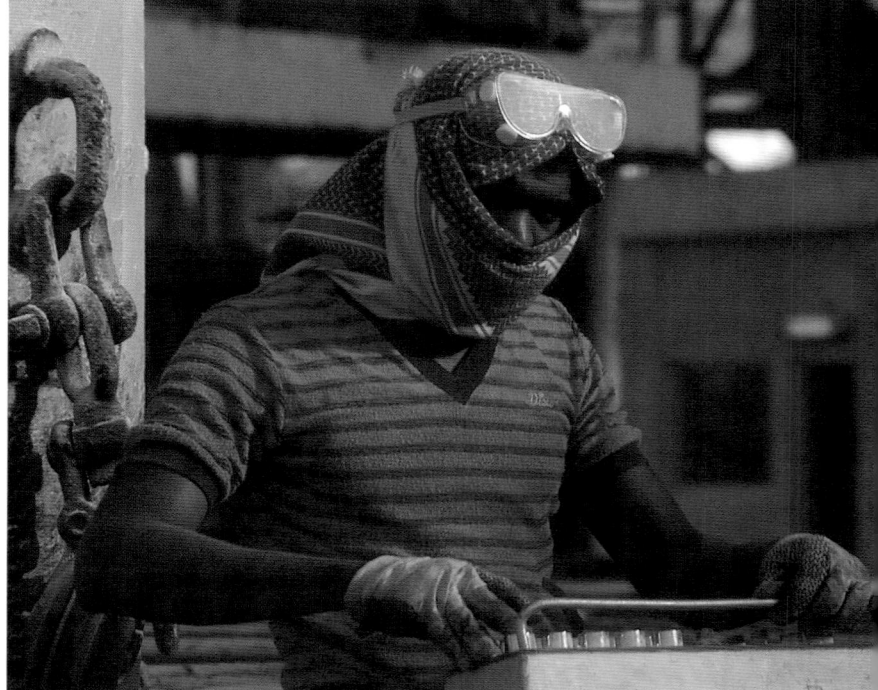

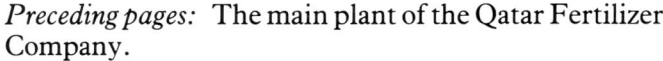

Preceding pages: The main plant of the Qatar Fertilizer Company.

This page: QAFCO produces ammonia and urea, which are loaded directly at the Company's jetty in Umm Said for export, especially to the Far East.

The Qatar Steel Company (QASCO) factory at Umm Said: unloading and carrying iron ore pellets to the plant (*top left*); the electric arc furnace (*right*) provides molten steel for the

continuous casting machines. Steel rods *(bottom left and centre)* ready for loading and export to neighbouring Gulf countries.

The light industrial area on the Salwa Road outside Doha, set up as part of the Government initiative to encourage private enterprise and diversification, houses a variety of successful small companies, producing, among others, detergent products *(left)*, dairy products and ice cream *(centre)*, and marine paints *(right)*.

A Government experimental farm in the north; with the aid of irrigation and advanced agricultural techniques the desert has been tamed and a large variety of crops and foodstuffs produced to meet domestic needs. The Government's long term aim is self-sufficiency in food production.

The demand for bank services has risen sharply since the oil price rises of 1973-4, and activity has expanded in this new field. Qatar now has sufficient banks to meet all local needs. The Qatar Monetary Agency (*above*) is the country's central bank authority. The Qatar National Bank (*left and right*) was set up in 1965, and continues to deal largely with Government deposits.

The economic boom and population increase have called for enormous expansion in the construction industry: in Doha vast offices (*centre left*) and public buildings, such as the new General Post Office (*top left*) continue to rise, and an efficient road network eases movement in the ever-growing city (*bottom left*). New towns have sprung up – Umm Said now has an impressive residential centre for workers in the industrial area (*above centre*). Qatar produces enough cement to provide for half the local demand, at Umm Bab in the south-west (*below centre*). Basic needs, for water and power are ever on the increase: the new power station at Ras Abu Fontas (*above*) has a vast generating capacity which fuels also the desalination units, providing an efficient supply of fresh water (*right*) for the capital. (*overleaf*) Major road construction programmes outside the capital are now substantially complete, linking all points of the country with fast, efficient carriageways.

133

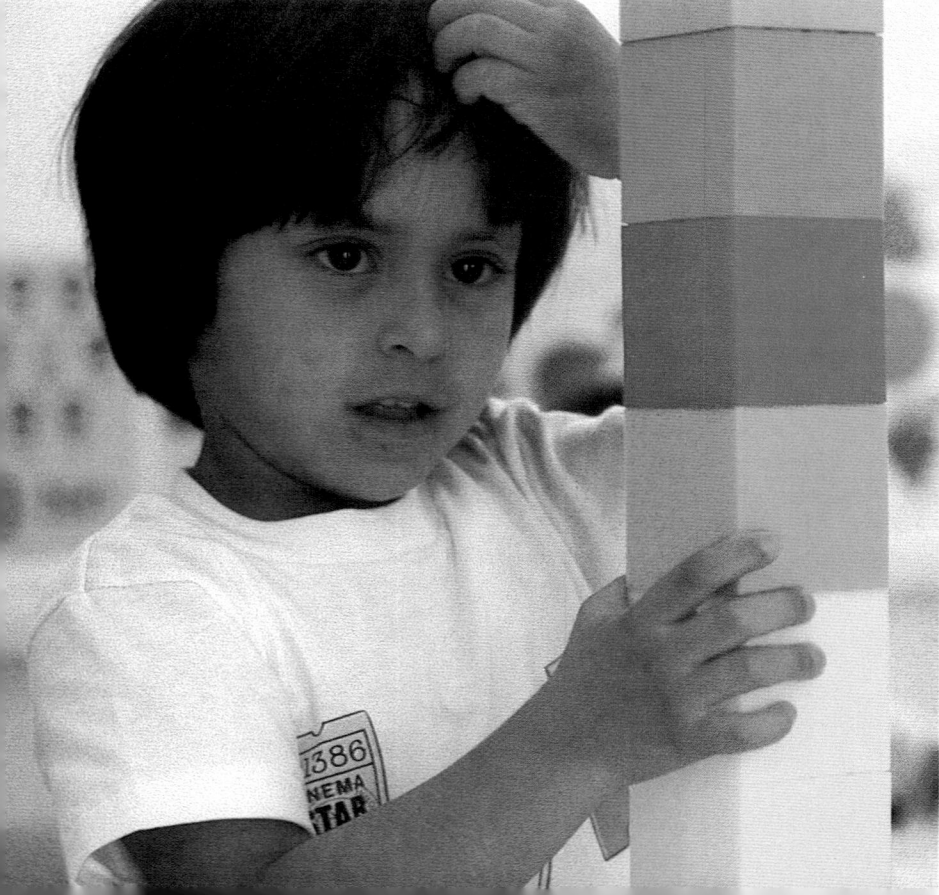

Preceding page: At a boys' secondary school in Doha.

These pages: A nursery school in a Doha suburb.

A primary school for boys, built recently in a new residential quarter of Doha, and typical of the many fully equipped schools set up throughout the country under the recent school building programme. Girls too benefit from these up-to-date facilities.

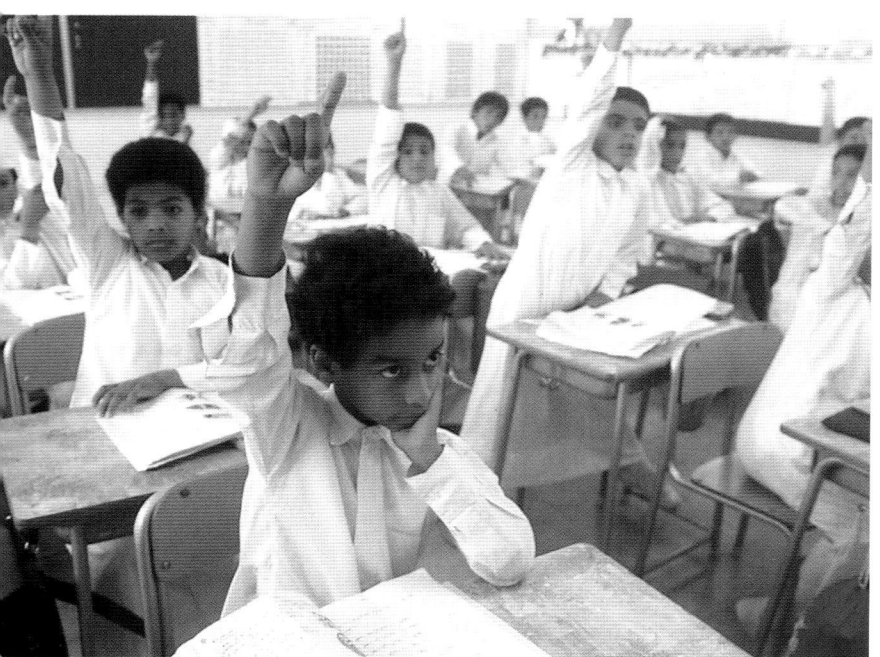

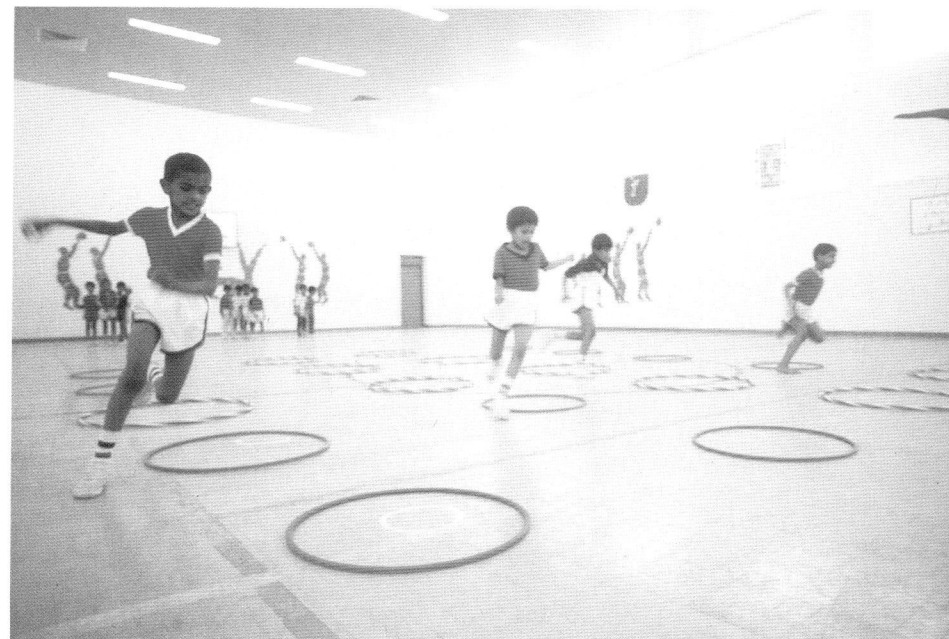

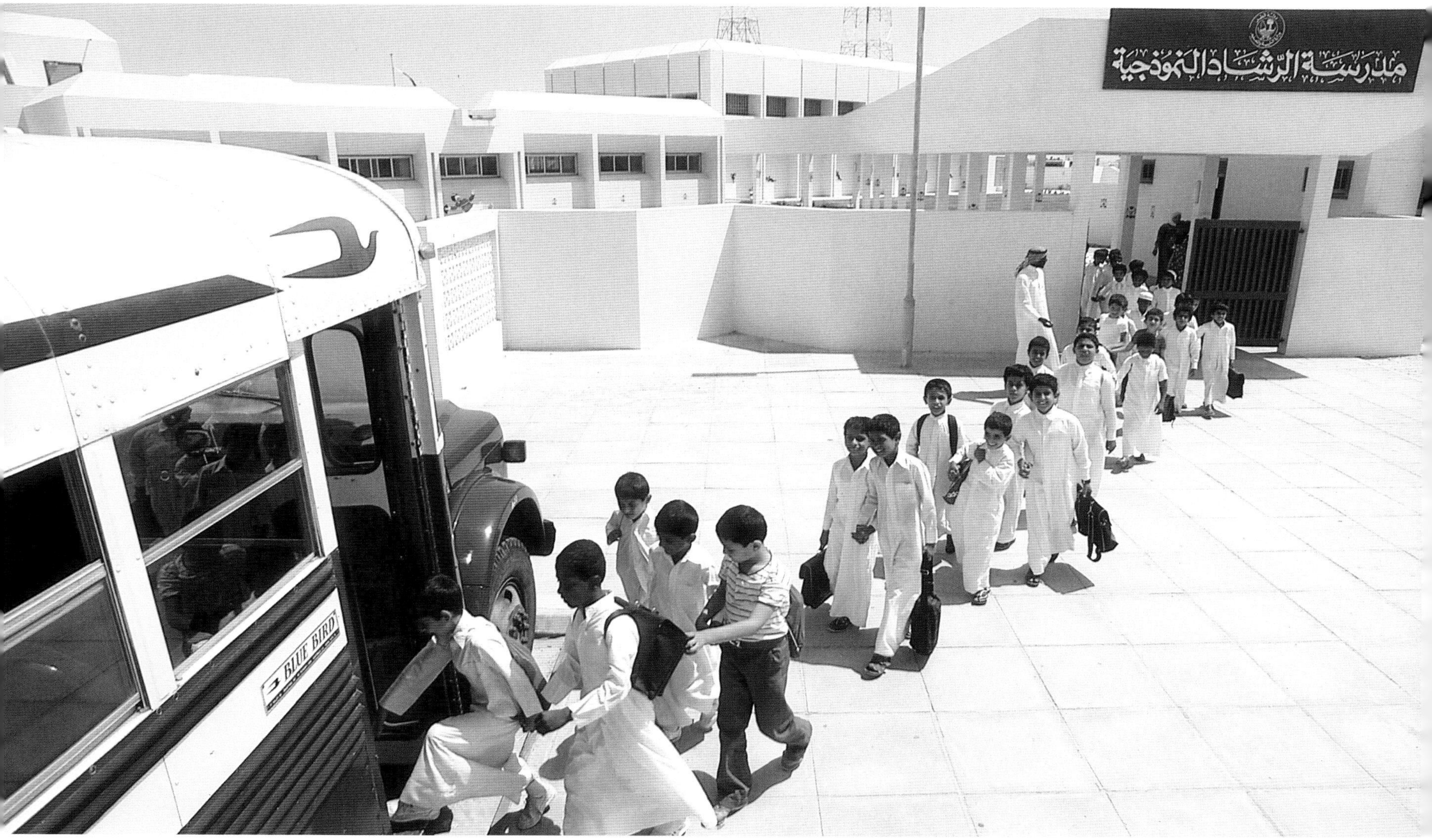
مدرسة الرشاد النموذجية
BLUE BIRD

Pupils in secondary education *(left)* may follow a number of specialised paths: scientific, literary, technical, commercial or religious. At a religious institute in Doha: library facilities *(centre)*; end-of-year examinations in progress *(right)*.

Overleaf: The distinctive wind towers are the dominant architectural motif of the new University of Qatar campus, to the north west of Doha.

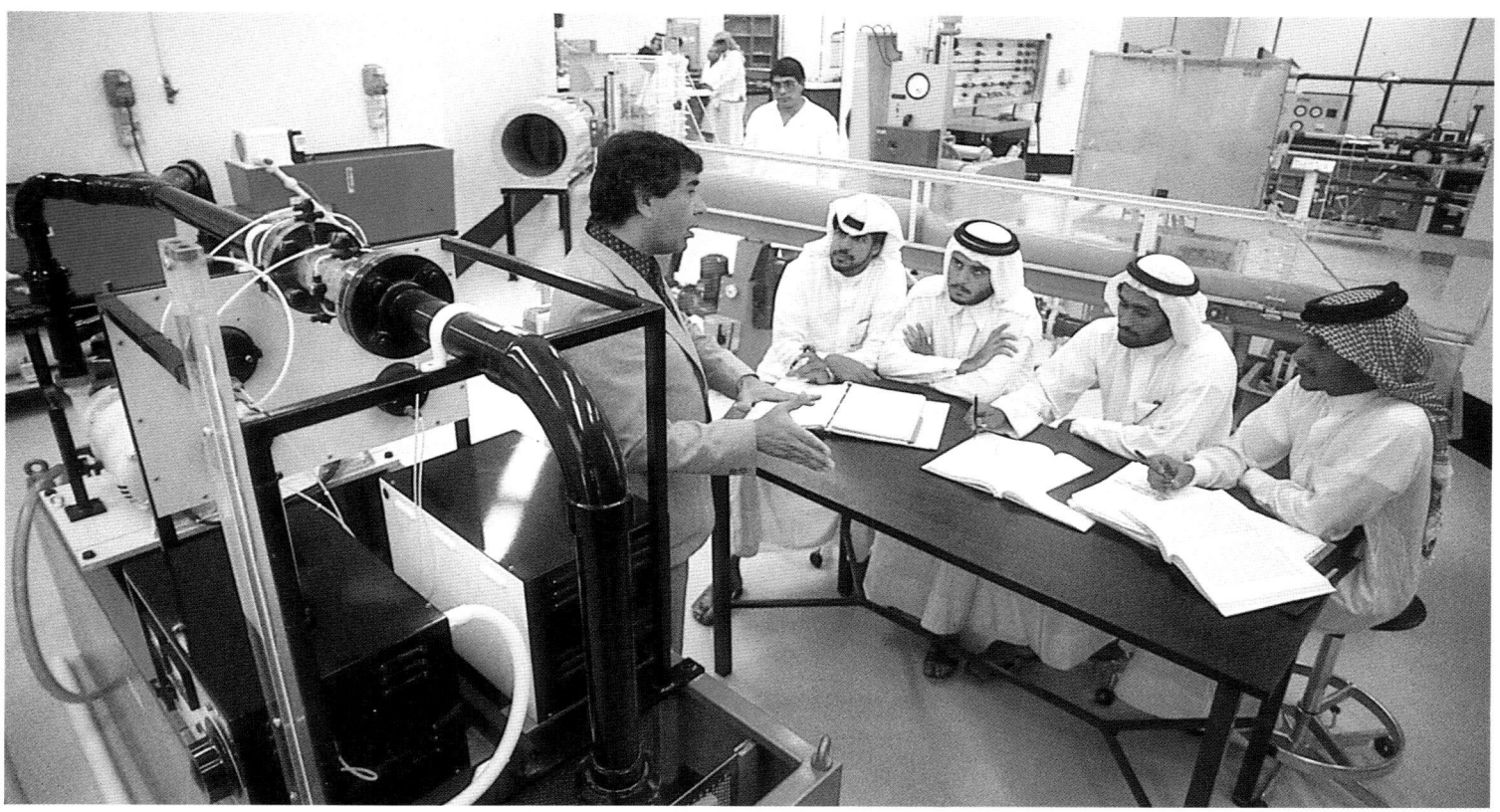

Students at the University of Qatar *(left)*; a class in progress in the Fluid Mechanics laboratory, Faculty of Engineering *(above)*; *(below)* students at work in the Computer Aided Design department.

The Doha Vocational Training Institute offers necessary practical training to international standards in a wide range of disciplines, for Qataris aiming to work in the country's technical and industrial sectors.

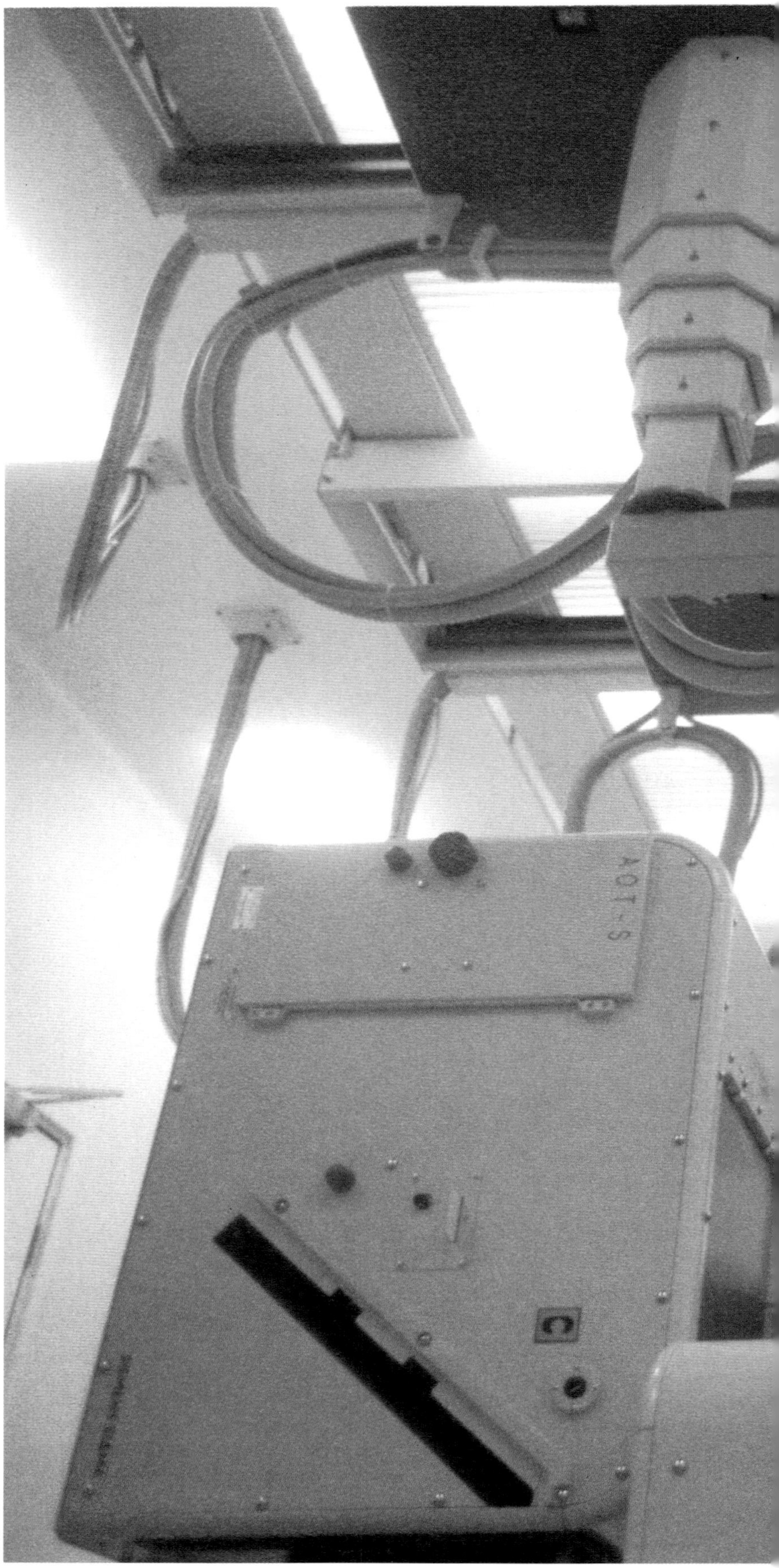

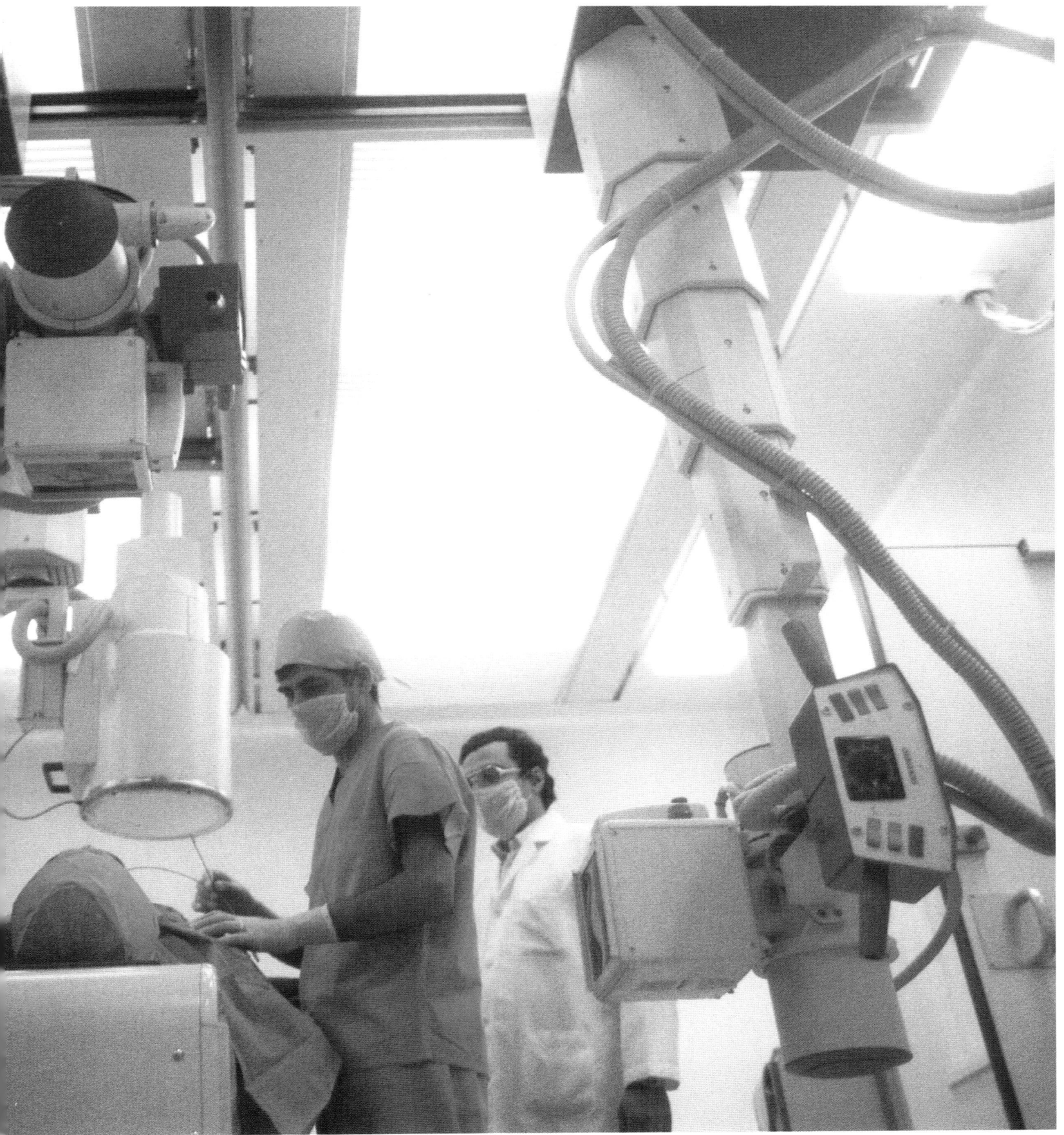

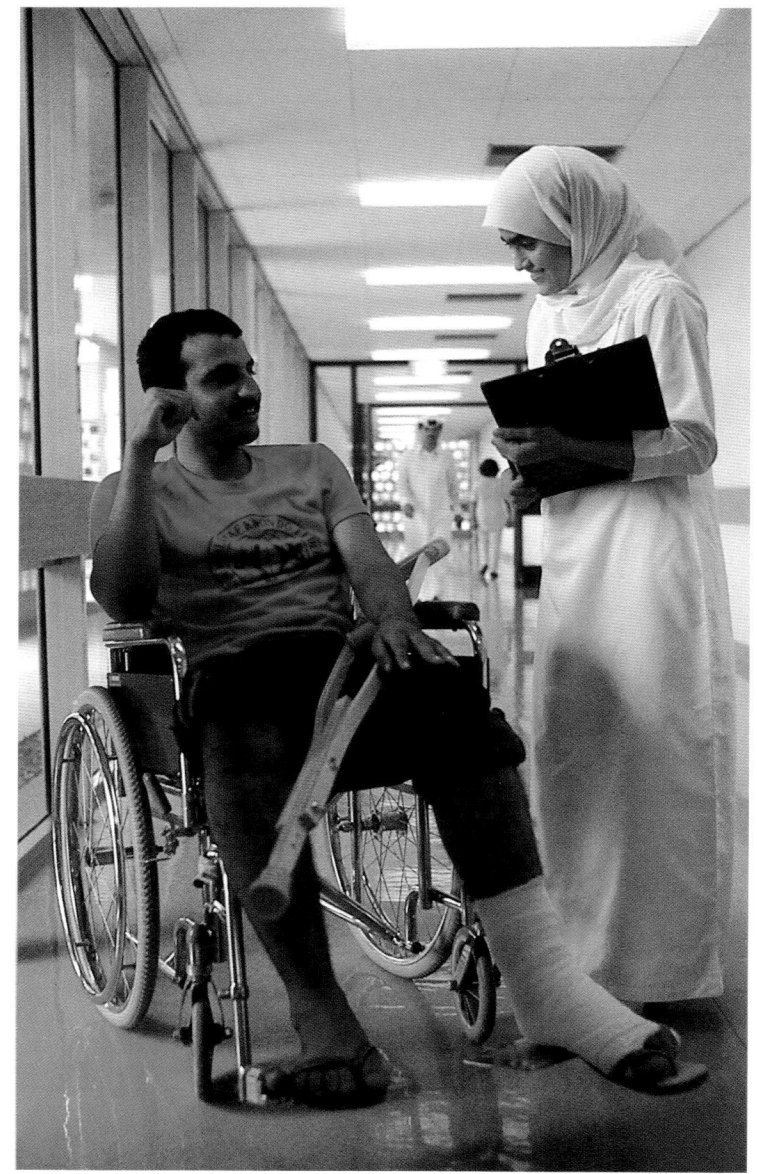

The Hamad General Hospital (*preceding pages, top and bottom left*), opened in 1983. The hospital provides one of the foremost comprehensive medical services in the Gulf region, making use of the most advanced medical technology on offer: (*preceding pages, right*) the angiography X-ray machine. Health care at a personal level is no less important at the hospital: child care (*below*); in the childrens' playroom (*below right*); an increasing proportion of the nursing staff is Qatari (*right*).

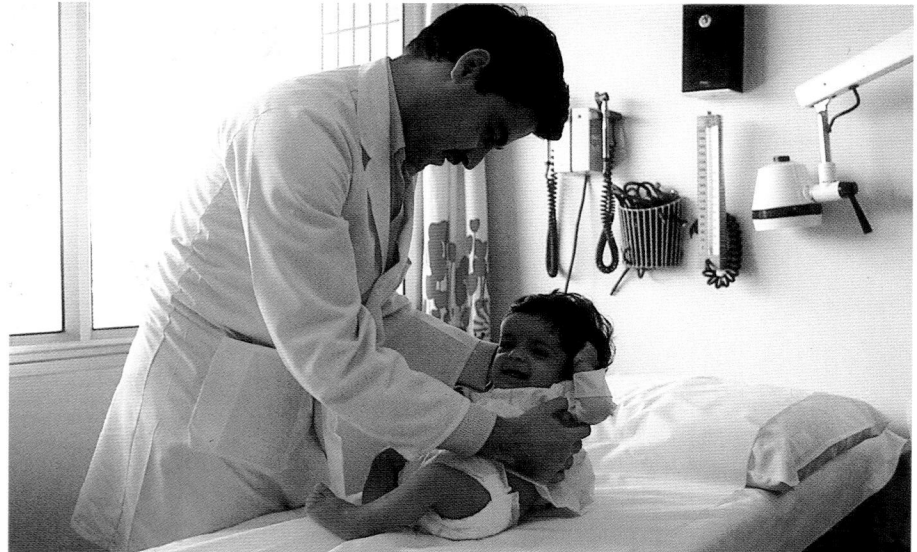

A national network of health services has been built up, and facilities continue to expand; *(above left)* the new National Women's Hospital in Doha, and a fully equipped local health centre at Dukhan in the west *(left and below)*.

Preceding page: The series of ring roads around Doha relieves traffic congestion in the city centre.
Doha Port at dusk.

While heavy industrial exports pass through the port at Umm Said, Doha Port *(below and right)* was expanded in the 1970s to enable it to carry most general cargo. There are plans for future expansion.

Overleaf: A Gulf Air Tristar comes down over the bay to land at Doha International Airport.

Qatar's largest earth satellite station, at Mukheinis in central Qatar, linked to Intelsat's satellites over the Indian and Atlantic oceans.

Doha from the air: enormous growth in recent decades has changed the city beyond recognition. Plans for future progress are equally ambitious.